Septuagenarian, Maureen Tyler lives with her husband in a small village on the Fylde Coast surrounded by fields and wildlife.

Maureen is a qualified drama teacher, of over 36 years, working closely with LAMDA both as a teacher and representative. She has been a member of two amateur drama groups,
both acting and directing.

For ten years, Maureen worked as a voice coach for the BBC Journalism Course at Lancashire University.

She is a keen golfer and enjoys reading – any genre. She has written poems from a very early age.

Animal Alphabet

A Series of Delightful Fun Poems

MAUREEN TYLER

AUSTIN MACAULEY PUBLISHERS™
LONDON · CAMBRIDGE · NEW YORK · SHARJAH

Copyright © Maureen Tyler (2018)

The right of **Maureen Tyler** to be identified as author of this work has been asserted by her in accordance with section 77 and 78 of the Copyright, Designs and Patents Act 1988.

All rights reserved. No part of this publication may be reproduced, stored in a retrieval system, or transmitted in any form or by any means, electronic, mechanical, photocopying, recording, or otherwise, without the prior permission of the publishers.

Any person who commits any unauthorised act in relation to this publication may be liable to criminal prosecution and civil claims for damages.

A CIP catalogue record for this title is available from the British Library.

ISBN 9781528912556 (Paperback)
ISBN 9781528912563 (Hardback)
ISBN 9781528912570 (E-Book)
www.austinmacauley.com

First Published (2018)

Austin Macauley Publishers Ltd

25 Canada Square

Canary Wharf

London

E14 5LQ

I would like to dedicate this book to my husband Dave,
without whom it would never have been sent to a publisher.
My lifelong friend and husband of 50 years.

My thanks to Rosalind Buckland for her inspiration on illustrating some of my early poems. Thanks to Rowan Collinge for the insight of a four-year-old. Also, thanks to Anna Cooper and the Production Team at Austin Macauley.

Amy the Armadillo

Amy the Armadillo
Is asleep on her pillow
And she's dreaming
Of eating the ants.

But she'd better beware
Cos Edward Bear
Has got them stuck
To the seat of his pants.

Anthony the Ant

Anthony the Ant
Wears bright blue pants
Which he bought
From the jumble sale.

Now on his feet
Looking ever so neat
He's wearing wellingtons
Bought from a whale.

BERTIE THE BEE

Bertie the Bee
Flies around saying, "WHEE!"
As he flutters
From flower to flower.

"This is great!" says he.
"I am Bertie the Bee
And I'm fitted
With TURBO POWER!"

BRENDA THE BEAR

**Brenda the Bear
Has got no hair.
She's lost an eye as well.
"But don't despair,"
says Edward Bear.
"I love you just as well."**

COLIN THE CAT

Colin the Cat has six meals a day.
He used to be thin, but he won't stay that way.
He likes fish, chicken, rabbit and lamb
But he turns his nose up when he's given Spam!

He lives on Number One Aristotle Street
And there he has breakfast each day of the week.
House Number Two is his next port of call
And after that, he jumps over the wall

To Mrs Jones, who lives at Number Three
And there he's in time for the afternoon tea.
At Number Four, he calls for a snack
Then lies fast asleep on the cosy doormat.

When he wakes up, he's off once again
And enters Number Five down the back lane.
He makes his home there for quite a while
And then decides it's supper time.

So off he pops to House Number Six
And pays for his supper with a couple of tricks.
Now after that, it's time for a nap
So, he curls fast asleep on his owner's lap.

Cuthbert the Cow

Cuthbert the cow
Just doesn't know how
To jump right over the moon.

When he ran up the path
The little dog laughed
And the dish ran away with the spoon.

DAISY THE DUCK

Daisy the Duck
Has run out of luck.
She can't get into the pond.

A large net is there
Not visible from air.
And she doesn't know where to land.

"It's one, two, three … Down!
I might hit the ground.
Or shall I just land on the net?

"Oh, I'll give it a go
Take it ever so slow
It doesn't matter, if I get my feet wet.

"Oh this is such fun
I'm sat down on my bum
Now I'm going back up in the air.

"It's really a treat
Now I'm back on my feet
And I'm bouncing around with no cares."

DANIEL THE DRAGON

Daniel the Dragon can't get to sleep.
He's tried and tried, for over a week.
Each time he feels his eyes start to shut
A funny feeling starts up in his foot.

It could be cramp, or it could be gout.
It hurts so much, he wants to shout,
"Oh, help me, someone! Get rid of the pain!
I'll be a good dragon and not breathe out flames!"

His friend, Albert, jumped up off his foot
And said he'd get better now he had stood up.
So Dan drifted off into a nice sleep
And didn't wake up for over a week.

Dido the dog

Dido the dog
Is stuck in the bog
As he watches
The day go by.

He looks left and right
But he never will bite
Cos deep down
He's really quite shy.

I think it's time
For me to shine
So I'll jump
Right out of this bog.

Now just wait and see
He's sat on the knee
Of a gentleman
That's just passed by!

Douglas the Dinosaur

Doug the dinosaur, was feeling quite glum.
He'd a terrible pain inside of his tum.
"Now, was it the fish or was it the beef
Or was it that funny looking green leaf?

They say greens are good for you.
Is that really true?
I'm not turning red or yellow but blue!
I think I'm going to be quite sick
Just turn around, please
I'll try to be quick!

Now fancy that. It wasn't the greens
Just that massive plateful of baked beans.
You'd better be careful. I might just burp.
You wouldn't want that mess all over your shirt."

ELLA THE ELEPHANT

Ella the elephant just loves to sing
As she soars in the air
On the elephant swing.
Higher and higher
Into the bright sky—
Now wait a minute
She's started to fly!

Her ears are flapping
Up and down
And now she's headed into town.

The crowd all gasp
As she flies past
Her voice cries out
Like a drum.

"Oh this is fun
Fun for everyone
Please join me
If you can!"

FERDY THE FLEA

Ferdy the Flea
Is just like me
As he loves to
Hop around.

He likes the cat
Sat on the mat
And just jumps
Upon his knee.

But the cat on the mat
Does NOT like that
And he scratches
Away at his knee.

So Ferdy the Flea
Jumps off his knee
And starts annoying
You and me!

FREDDY THE FROG

**Freddy the Frog
Hopped over the log
As he tried to keep up
In the race.**

**But poor Freddy fell flat
But not on his back
And now he's got mud
On his face!**

GEORGE THE GIRAFFE

George the Giraffe
Just loves to laugh
As he eats the leaves
From the trees.

He's ever so tall
But his baby is small
And only reaches
Up to his knees.

Now George bends down,
Down to the ground
And he gently gives
Baby a squeeze.

Now baby jumps round
On the dirty, dusty ground
When all of a sudden
He gives a big SNEEZE!

So, George just laughs
At baby giraffe
As he wriggles
Around in the leaves.

Godwin the Goose

Godwin the Goose,
Friend of Morris the Moose,
Says to Morris,
"Why do you always despair?
At least, you've got one tooth
Not like me and our Ruth
And you've also got lovely white hair."

Henry the Hedgehog

**Henry the Hedgehog
Is asleep on the log,
When the sun comes
Out in the day.**

**So he rolls off the log
Does Henry Hedgehog
And decides to
Go out and play.**

Iris the Ibis

Iris the Ibis
Is a sweet little bird.
She lives in the swamp
And can often be heard
When the rain comes tumbling down.

It's wet in the swamp
It's dark
And it's damp
But Iris still loves to tweet.

She's not bothered a bit
Cos her wellies do fit
Nice and snuggly upon
Her sweet feet.

JIMMY THE JACKAL

Jimmy the Jackal
Is really quite tall
And lives in the
Forest and woods.

But you'd better beware
If he finds you there
Because he isn't
As nice as he looks.

His teeth are sharp
As the fishing carp
And he's likely to
Give a left hook.

So, stay out of there
And do take care
Just peer in and
Take a look!

KATIE THE KITTEN

Katie the kitten
Has got pink ribbons
Tied up on the
Top of her head.

She looks ever so neat
Soft, fluffy and sweet
And just ready to
Tuck up in bed.

KIM THE KANGAROO

**Kim the Kangaroo
Is stuck in the zoo.
She'd rather be out in the town.**

**The sun is bright blue
"Now what shall I do?"
She really is feeling quite down.**

**She says to her mate
"It's getting rather late
I'll never get into the town."**

**Skip says to young Kim,
"You really are dim.
You just haven't got the right gown."**

LAWRENCE THE LION

**Lawrence the Lion
Has got out his iron
To put creases
Into his pants.**

**But he'd better take care
Or he'll burn all his hair
If he irons them
While they're still on.**

LUCY THE LAMB

Lucy the Lamb
Loves strawberry jam
And she spreads it
On toast every day.
It gets in her hair.
It gets everywhere!
And she doesn't know
What to say.
"I'd best give it up
I'm such a daft pup
I'm really a stupid ass.
I'll do what I can.
Not eat strawberry jam.
I'll just stick to boring old grass."

MOLLY THE MOUSE

**Molly the Mouse
Is asleep in her house
Nestled quietly
Under the stairs.**

**Don't make a peep
And disturb her nice sleep
Cos she's dreaming
Of apples and pears.**

MORRIS THE MOOSE

**Morris the Moose
Has got a tooth loose
And he wiggles it round
With his tongue.**

**But he'd better take care
It's still held by a hair
And now his tongue
Is extremely long.**

Norman the Newt

Norman the Newt
Has got a new suit.
And he looks very smart
And debonair.

But the problem with that
Is he's to wear a hat
As he's not got
Any hair.

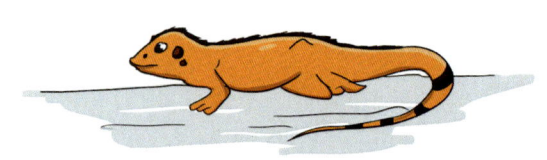

Olly the Octopus

**Olly the Octopus
Lives in the sea
And his best friend
Is Ferdy the Flea.**

**They splash around
Making lots of sound
And they're annoying
To you and to me!**

Oswald the Ostrich

Oswald the Ostrich
Just doesn't know which
Way to turn
With his head
Stuck into the ground.

His bum's stuck in the air
But he just doesn't care
That he can't
Seem to get
The right way around.

So Kim Kangaroo
Off home to the zoo
And wearing her brand new gown,
Says to Oswald
"Wait there.
I'll go get the chair
The one I've only just found."

Now Kim stands up tall
But she's still too small
To get Oswald
To pull his head out.

So she gives him a push.
He comes out in a rush
And continues to run
Round and around.

Priscilla the Pig

Priscilla the Pig
Is really quite big,
And she's standing alone
In her sty.

She's full of the blues
She can't find her new shoes
And her feet are so cold.
I don't know why?

Queenie the Quadrasaurapod

Queenie the Quadrasaurapod
Is married to the policeman
Called Mr Plod.

She's really quite helpful
When things go wrong
Because her four feet
Are especially long.

She's great at chasing
Down the road
In timely pursuit of
Mr boastful Toad.

He's stolen Noddy's little car,
Which is quite a shame,
But Queenie is a match
For his naughty game.

She belts down the road
After Mr Toad
And soon overtakes him
With his stolen load.

For Noddy's car came to a stop
And out of the car
Mr Toad does hop.
He says he's sorry
With a great big grin.
But Queenie just knocks him
On his chin.

"You are naughty, Mr Toad,"
Queenie says to him
On the road.
"Next time you feel you
You want a ride
I'm more than willing
To oblige.

"Just pop around
To Mr Plod,
My handsome quadrasaurapod,
And ask him politely
For a ride,
As I said,
I'm happy to oblige!"

Quentin the Queenie

Quentin the Queenie
Is ever so tweeny
As he nestles deep down
In his shell.

"Will I ever grow big
Like Priscilla the Pig?
Did she start her life
In a shell?"

Mum looked at her Queenie
And smiled so serenely
And said, "I don't know about that
She is really quite fat and
I don't think she'd fit
Into a shell."

"Oh, that's okay," says Queenie
"I think I'll stay tweeny
I don't want to grow out
Of my shell."

Renee the Rabbit

Renee the Rabbit
Is not very good
She is constantly
Picking her nose.

Her mother said,
"That's not very good
You'd be better
Concentrating
On your toes!"

Robin the Rhinoceros

Robin the Rhinoceros
Just loves to swim.
Even though they say
He's really quite dim.

He paddles around
With his nose in the air
And floats around
Without any care.

But then he'll decide
To turn onto his back
And finesse he certainly
Does not lack.

He zooms up and down
The muddy hot stream.
He'll soon be in
The Olympic Team.

ROGER THE RAT

Roger the Rat
Is asleep on the mat
And the cat is away
Down his hole.

The cows in the trees,
Not disturbing the breeze
And poor Robin's alone
With the Mole.

The hen's in the pen
Playing cards with the men,
And the pig's pecking corn
On his own.

The dog's in the stable
And her name is Mabel
And the horse chews away
On his bone.

And I sit on the peas
With the pods on my knees
And they're taking me away
To a HOME.

Sam the Spider

Sam the Spider
Got stuck in the jar
And tried to get out
But couldn't get far.

He cried and cried
With lots of tears
And was glad he'd been
Swimming
For so many years.

The jar filled up
Right up to the top
So he swam his way up
And jumped out with a hop.

SAMUEL THE SLUG

Samuel the Slug
Just wants a big hug.
He's fed up of just
Sludging around.

He sets off up the path
And the birds all do laugh,
As his body is
Stuck to the ground.

"We'll lift you up
With a great big hup
Tied to the end
Of a rope."

"We can't have that,
I'll look like a Rat
On the end of
A garden hose!"

SEBASTIAN THE SKUNK

Sebastian the Skunk
Has got loads of spunk
And he fights with
Such flash and such flare!

He spins round and round
With his feet off the ground
And his sword held up
High in the air!

He lunges just right
With all of his might
His opponent just looks
And just stares.

He's not scared of the Skunk,
Cos Seb's dressed as a Punk!
He's got purple and pink
In his hair!

SIDNEY THE SNAIL

Sidney the Snail
Is small and brown.
His house keeps him warm
When it rains.

He lives in a garden
That's full of flowers
And lots to eat
For hours and hours.

But he has to be careful
When the birds are around
They all think nothing
Of smashing him into the ground!

STANLEY THE STOAT

**Stanley the Stoat's
Got a lump in his throat
Caused by eating a
Slimy green toad.**

**When he opens his mouth
He hardly can shout
All he can do
Is just CROAK!**

TERENCE THE TOAD

Terence the Toad
Just loves it
When he's on the road.

But unfortunately
He doesn't own a car.

Which doesn't get him very far!

He has this habit,
Or so I'm told,
To steal any car.
He is so bold.

But this is really
Not very good
When he comes across
A quadrasaurapod!

THOMAS THE TIGER

Thomas the Tiger, with eyes so bright
Goes hunting when it's late at night.
He opens his mouth and lets out a roar
And thunders around on the sun-baked floor.

But he doesn't find a bite to eat
And says, "I'll think I'll go to sleep.
Hunting at night is not much fun.
Especially when you're only ONE!"

Toby the Turtle

Toby the Turtle
Was short, fat and round.
Yes, Toby was a turtle
And lived on things he found.

He liked to munch an apple core
But was careful with the pips,
And when he found a chunk of cheese
He drooled and licked his lips.

Yes, Toby was a turtle,
Very fat, short and round.
And when he'd finished eating
His belly would touch the ground.

TREVOR THE TADPOLE

Trevor the Tadpole
Swims round in the pond.
His head is quite big
But his tail, it grows long.

Now it's ever so neat,
He's grown four small webbed feet
And he's changed to a
Lovely bright green.

He jumps out with a hop,
He just cannot stop
And laze all day long
In the pond.

He's a tadpole no more.
He can jump round the floor.
And now he's happy the
Whole day long.

URMA THE UNICORN

Urma the Unicorn
Has got a long horn
Right in the middle
Of her head.

It's alright through the day
But it gets in the way
When it's time
To get ready for bed.

Vernon the Viper

Vernon the Viper
Is not very nice.
Cos when he's hungry
He eats lots of mice.

Now some may like that
With sugar and spice,
But I like them savoury
With chicken and rice!

Walter the Worm

Walter the Worm
Just loves to squirm,
And his body
Is all squidgy and soft.

He's tied onto a hook,
And it's just his bad luck,
He is swung to and fro
Up aloft.

He pulls himself up,
To escape from the hook,
And wiggles himself
All around.

With a mighty heave
He finds himself free
And with a PLOP!
He falls to the ground.

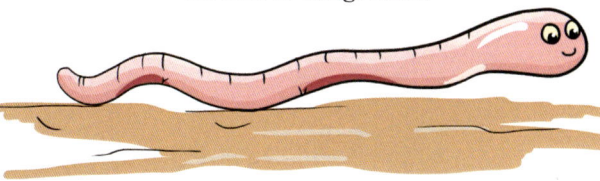

Wilma the Weasel

Wilma the Weasel
Has got a measle
Right on the end
Of her nose.

"How did it get there?
I always take care
To breathe deeply
When sniffing a rose."

XAVIER THE X-RAY TETCHA

Xavier the X-ray Tetcha,
Said, "By gosh, by golly, I betcha.
I can see you, but you can't see me
When we're swimming in the sea."

YORICK THE YAK

Yorick the Yak
Has very long hair
And he lives in Tibet
In the family's lair.

He's very rude
When he's eating his food
And his teeth are so
Strikingly white.

But you'd better beware
If you stand and stare.
Cos he's likely
To give you a bite.

Zara the Zebra

**Zara the Zebra
Is really quite sweet.
She has lots of flowers
At her feet.
And when she chases around the
zoo
We can see she's happy.
(We are too!)**

Zumba the Zonkey

Zumba the Zonkey.
His mother's a donkey
And his father's all
Covered in stripes.

He just loves to dance,
When he gets the chance,
And his long black tail
Swings from side to side.

He can travel for miles
Out in the wilds
As he searches the lands
Far and wide.

But you'd better take care
He's not like a bear.
And he won't EVER
Give you a ride!